BLUEPRINT
of a
Kingdom
BUSINESS

Seek first!
Matt 6:33

Ernest F. Parrish

BLUEPRINT OF A KINGDOM BUSINESS

DISCOVERING REDEMPTIVE VALUE IN YOUR BUSINESS CALLING

By
E. F. Parrish

CEDAR GATE
PUBLISHING

Blueprint of a Kingdom Business

Unless otherwise noted, scripture quotations are taken from the New International Version of the Bible.

THE HOLY BIBLE, NEW INTERNATIONAL VERSION®
NIV®
Copyright © 1973, 1978, 1984 by International Bible Society®
Used by permission. All rights reserved worldwide.

ISBN-13: 978-0999711798

Content Editor: Kim Mullens
Edited by Nancy Parrish & Mackenzie Richardson
Cover design: Scott Soliz

Printed in the United States of America

Endorsements

"When business is done God's way, there should be a line of applicants wanting to work for these loving leaders. Boe writes an inspiring book that gives the practical examples we so desperately need to help us see what is possible. But I will warn you, only implement these biblical principles if you want to change the world around you."

— FRANK SMITH, president of *Mosaic Personnel Solutions* and *Driving Happiness at Work*

"This book is the best resource I've ever seen to inspire business owners and leaders to see their workplaces as a mission field! Boe's decades of corporate chaplaincy have resulted in countless stories of transformation and life changes; many of which are shared in this book. If you are a business owner or leader, this is a must read. Be prepared to be inspired to build a kingdom business and leave a lasting legacy!"

— ADAM BARNETT, lead pastor at *Redeemer Church* in Tulsa, Oklahoma

"Boe Parrish's background in both ministry and business, prior to becoming a corporate chaplain and forming a chaplaincy organization, and his subsequent devotion to helping people through their greatest trials and victories has given him great insight for the writing of a *Blueprint of a Kingdom Business*. In each chapter, you will find not only great stories of the help a corporate chaplain can be to the people that serve organizations, but real life examples and instructions on how to build a time tested and biblically sound God honoring kingdom business."

— STEVE TRICE, founder and Chairman of the Board for *Jasco Products Company*

"*Blueprint of a Kingdom Business* is a wonderful collection of stories and thoughts from a man who truly lives out the principles he outlines in the book. Boe Parrish eloquently puts into words some easy to follow steps on how to be a kingdom business owner. Follow the 'blueprint' and you will undoubtedly have a powerful kingdom impact!"

— STEVE FOSKIN, president of *CrossFirst Bank* in Oklahoma City

"Boe Parrish's personal experience in the corporate world, and in the ministry world, are beautifully combined to inspire any kingdom minded business owner. He tells practical stories that have made huge kingdom impact. After all, 'It is not about building a big business, it is about building big people.' I have worked beside Boe and can testify to the fact that this guy is the REAL DEAL and totally lives kingdom minded in all he does. I highly recommend this book as well as Corporate Care Inc's chaplaincy program to make a difference in your company."

— ROXANNE PARKS, author, speaker, certified life coach, president of *Winter Summit Ministries Inc*

Dedication

To my college sweetheart Nancy, who became my love-ly wife of nearly 44 years. She has believed in me and allowed me to dream dreams and pursue them with all my might. She makes me a much better writer than I really am.

Additionally, my three beautiful daughters Sarah, Jenifer and Laura and the amazing men they married Josh, Wyatt and Ty, and of course those fabulous grand-children Isaiah, Preston, Lydia and Julia. Every one of you have been a huge blessing to me and have inspired me and encouraged me to always go for it! This book is part of me going for it! I dedicate this book to you!

Table of Contents

FOREWORD

Boe and I were in our usual seats at the coffee shop one morning in May 2005. Conversation always included stupid jokes, prayer requests, and stories about our families and work. This particular morning, we were discussing what it would take to rebrand and rebirth a Corporate Care makeover. We ended our conversation with the commitment to pray about those important decisions. The following January, we launched the new look of Corporate Care. In doing so, we agreed to partner in the effort and solidified the partnership with a handshake and a prayer. Now, over fourteen years later, we enjoy our partnership and the opportunities it brings us, as corporate chaplains, to change the world!

Early in the process we thought it would be a good idea to draw up some company values and mark them non-negotiable. We called them the "Rules of the Game". They are as follows:

- Our work grows out of our meaningful relationships. Our business grows as a result of our attention to and care of these relationships.
- Our work reflects the character of God and attracts others with the aroma of Christ in all that we do.
- Our business focuses on equipping others,

giving them what they need to find their place.

- Our financial success blesses others and honors God and his Word.

Boe and I met in college at Oklahoma Baptist University when he arrived on campus as a freshman baseball player. I was a senior and we became friends that year. However, we lost track of each other following my senior year and connected again years later when we both served on different church staffs in Edmond. It wasn't much later when that conversation about corporate chaplaincy took place and changed our lives forever.

I am now in my forty-fifth year of ministry. The last fourteen as a corporate chaplain have been, by far, the most effective and fruitful. That effectiveness is due to our desire to please and honor God in all that we do. Boe leads the way. His heart reflects God's character and the love of his Savior, Jesus. He is zealous about discipling men who will disciple other men.

If you want to make a difference in the lives of people, there is no more effective way to do so than corporate chaplaincy. If you own a business, or want to own one someday in the future, placing a corporate chaplain among your employees will be the best investment you will make in the men and women with whom you work.

In his book, *Blueprint of a Kingdom Business*, Boe will help you understand what it means to make a difference in the lives of people, especially when they work for you. Read every page. Don't miss a detail. Go make a difference!

Jon Cook

Partner of Corporate Care, Inc.

Edmond, Oklahoma

Chapter 1

Beginning a Ministry in Business

And let us consider how to stir up one another to love and good works.   Hebrews 10:24

My professional career dream path did not include becoming a corporate chaplain. As a matter of fact, there were no corporate chaplains in the late 1970's at all. Upon finishing our college careers at Oklahoma Baptist University, my wife and I began serving seven years in local church ministry. Suddenly, the opportunities dried up before my very eyes. It was then I found myself thrust into the business world for the first time.

An opportunity to go into sales presented itself and I found great success over the next few years. After achieving in sales more than I ever thought possible, I was presented with my next business opportunity: managing salespeople. Wholeheartedly, I poured my life into this new level of business challenge. Again, I was blessed with wonderful success. During this season, when I was outside of full-time vocational ministry, I realized that ministry was a lifestyle to live, not a position or office to be held.

Opportunity after opportunity began to spring up for ministry in the marketplace. Salespeople with broken lives, clients facing all kinds of challenges, and company executives just needing someone they could vent to, knowing their privacy would be respected. All of these activities contributed to the genesis idea of Corporate Care. The Lord was seeding my spirit with an idea of ministry in the marketplace, and I could hardly contain my excitement.

God revealed tremendous needs in the business world at all levels. People needed encouragement, hope, and direction from someone they knew and trusted. It wasn't long after when my friend, Scott Lewis, approached me, having a similar vision for marketplace ministry. We met at a Hardee's restaurant in Edmond, Oklahoma over a weekend, and mapped out what corporate chaplaincy might look like. We scribbled on napkins for two days in this little fast food restaurant back in September 1987, combining my two greatest passions; business and ministry. Corporate Care was born! I still have those napkins in a file all these years later. God was faithful to allow me to see all of the dreams we jotted down so many years ago, come to fruition. What a blessing it's been from God to walk with some of the nation's greatest business leaders, pouring into their lives the presence of our Father.

After incorporating the business as a regular C Corp., we were off to the races trying to find our first clients. Scott and I had a mutual friend whose family owned a food distribution business, and he asked Scott to come and be his corporate chaplain. It was almost one year later when I found my first client, and they have remained a client for over thirty-two years. It has been a remarkable journey, witnessing the gospel being lived in front of businesspeople, with over 1200 employees and business owners coming to know Christ where they initiated the conversation. God directed us not to enter a business as an evangelist, but always as a servant and a chaplain. We only have the "God talk" if we are invited to go there by the employees or the employer. It's the ultimate moment to lead someone to Christ if we are invited to do so. It does not matter if someone is Baptist or Buddhist, Muslim or Methodist, we care equally for each person. Every employee is a priceless treasure and deserves to be cared for with the highest standards and complete confidentiality.

As I reflect back over the last thirty-three years, there are very few regrets. This path of ministry has been the most exciting and fulfilling ministry of my life. I wouldn't change one day of this career path God laid out for me. I believe the Father has uniquely customized my ministry track. He knows my heart and my gifts even better than I do. He's allowed me to be a guide through life with tens of thousands of employees, employers, and chaplains! We have done this through relative obscurity, which honestly, is exactly the way I would've planned it. However, I didn't plan it, it has all been done by God's hand for His glory!

One of the key benefits I have gained as a result of walking through America's companies the last three decades, is discovering several great kingdom business owners along the way, and watching them live their faith in front of their employees, vendors, and community in quite profound ways. I have been privileged to sit at the tables of many great business executives, observing and contributing to transforming their business cultures into kingdom cultures which ignited redeeming values, transforming lives forever! Men and women who came to realize they could have a business vision as passionate and eternal as their pastor's vision. Business owners could lead their companies into transformed lives just as effectively as any clergyman. In fact, these business owners realized they hold the key to the local church's greatest mission field: They discovered redemptive value in their business calling.

A major paradigm shift occurs when they discover that God did not give them all these people to build a big business, rather He gave them a business to build big people! That is the game changer. I would love to share some stories of how this remarkable journey transpired. Buckle up and get ready to read some of the most exciting stories you'll ever hear, from the heroes of this book, the kingdom business owners who are making an eternal impact. Are you ready to begin your journey? I am here to help you be the next kingdom hero!

Chapter 2

Seeing Through the Smoke

They don't care how much you know, until they know how much you care.

The stage of my story begins in Oklahoma in the 1980's. Oklahomans lived in what would be ten roller coaster years of history, through the most prosperous decade of the twentieth century and the most depressed since the dust bowl. In 1981, it was the first year the word "internet" was mentioned. IBM released their first personal computer and Ronald Reagan was president. The inflation rate was over ten percent, and the average cost of a new house was 78,000 dollars. Oklahoma had enjoyed an oil boom that soared at its peak until 1982. As one oilman reflected in his later years, "The oil industry just ran over a cliff one night."

My story begins in August of 1983, after Penn Square Bank had fallen. When the bank fell in the summer of 1982, that was considered one of the most harmful actions for the state's economy and reputation. Money was scarce. The fall of Penn Square Bank had a domino effect causing other banks and Savings and Loans to close their doors on a daily basis.

The mega church we attended had a drop of over fifty percent in their income in a span of ninety days, without losing any families. People were scared. Money had evaporated before our eyes. Not one business, church, nonprofit, or government agency went untouched by the economic collapse.

During this economic backdrop, I decided to enter the marketplace and sell a capital expense item door to door, business to business, in Oklahoma City. What on earth was I thinking? I had accepted a job offer with a small office equipment dealership to sell copiers, printers, and fax machines. Businesses were trying to hold on for dear life and ride out the financial hurricane. No one in the business market wanted to spend money on anything, much less on depreciating office equipment. Yet, there I was, like the guy we've all seen reporting in the middle of the hurricane, hanging on and bracing himself so as not to get blown away.

The sales position was straight commission. If I didn't sell, I didn't eat. I was one of ten new salespeople who all started the same day. The current sales team was celebrating a huge monthly win by lighting up gargantuan cigars in the conference room. As I looked across the room, trying to raise my head above the cloud of smoke, I thought, "This is no place for a man of God." I felt like I should have been at the church working on staff, not fighting my way through cigar smoke in a conference room. Little did I know, in that smoke-filled moment, my destiny was sitting right in front of me.

The Lord was building my character foundation during those small everyday sales days. It was preparation for a much larger role. In my industry, most successful sales careers lead to sales management. I was blessed to have worked with a couple of Fortune 100 companies; one in the office equipment industry and the other in tele-communications. During the time I was a district sales manager, I managed multiple locations in several states. That brought me into the genesis of my destiny. I in-herited a group of dysfunctional salespeople. In fact, the district ranked 114th out of 116 districts nationally. It was my job to turn things around and inspire this district to move up in the rankings.

You can imagine what the sales representatives felt like, knowing they were at the bottom of the heap. I began caring for them as valued team members and as individuals. Guess what happened? They all started to produce. This wasn't an overnight success where ev-erything changed instantly. It was a consistent change though, and the transformation had begun. Over the next fifteen months, we went from worst to first! God blessed the work, and the idea of combining my two passions of business and ministry began. One of the most important lessons I learned was, "They don't care how much you know, until they know how much you care."

Chapter 3

WISDOM FROM PROVERBS

He who walks with the wise grows wise. But a companion of fools suffers harm. Proverbs 13:20

God directed my focus, during this time in my life, to be firmly planted in the book of Proverbs. I studied this book for sixty months. Yes, that's five years! He taught me business principles I never knew existed in the Bible. Reading through with the lens of the marketplace determined my focus. There were several principles I learned while studying Proverbs.

"All hard work brings a profit, but mere talk leads only to poverty" (Proverbs 14:23).

"Those who work their land will have abundant food, but those who chase fantasies lack judgment" (Proverbs 12:11).

"Diligent hands will rule, but laziness ends in slave labor" (Proverbs 12:24).

"Plans fail for lack of counsel, but with many advisors they succeed" (Proverbs 15:22).

"Commit to the Lord whatever you do and your plans will succeed" (Proverbs 16:3).

"Kings take pleasure in honest lips, and they value a man who speaks the truth" (Proverbs16:13).

"Whoever gives heed to instruction prospers" (Proverbs 16:20).

"A man of perverse heart does not prosper" (Proverbs 17:20).

"The first to present his case seems right until another comes forward and questions him" (Proverbs 8:17).

"The plans of the diligent lead to profit" (Proverbs 21:5).

"A generous man himself will be blessed, for he has shared his food with the poor" (Proverbs 22:9).

"Do you see a man skilled in his work? He will serve before kings, not obscure men" (Proverbs 22:29).

"A wise man has great power. A man of knowledge increases strength for waging war. You need guidance for victory" (Proverbs 24:5).

Little did I know how much these guiding biblical principles would be needed in the years to come. Daily, I would draw wisdom from the wealth of knowledge God was showing me in Proverbs. Many times, I had opportunities to compromise myself and my principles, little things that no one would see. I knew those were moments for me to live my life with integrity because God would see. Remember, *honesty* is what others see us doing; *integrity* is what we do when no one is looking.

Marketplace ministry had been birthed in my heart, and my life became all about this concept: The ministry of providing kingdom principles to business owners and their company employees through the chaplaincy program. Through Corporate Care we've been able to touch thousands of lives in the marketplace.

Chapter 4

INFLUENCE *IS* RELATIONSHIPS

John Maxwell says that leadership is influence. E.F. Parrish says that influence is relationships.

There is nothing wrong with managing a bottom line. We all have to do that, or we don't have a venue or platform to speak from. Many people want to discover how to use their business to build the kingdom of God while managing the bottom line, but don't know how to get there. My purpose has been to help business owners realize what kingdom business owners do differently. Throughout this book, I will continue to share stories and lessons I have learned as I stepped into the calling God prepared for me. Even during one of the darkest times in Oklahoma's history, God stepped in and changed my history to make it "His-story."

God has to be number one in everything we do. In a kingdom business, everything starts with Matthew 6:33, "But seek first his kingdom and his righteousness, and all these things will be added to you." God has to be number one in everything you think, do and say.

For years, it has been said that everything rises and falls on leadership. Whether you have a kingdom business or not, your business depends on leadership. When you seek a kingdom business model, there must be a paradigm shift. God did not give you all of these people to build a big business; rather, God gave you a business to build big people. This is a critical shift in thinking. For most business owners it is a foreign concept, shifting from profits to people seems backwards. Your eyes have to be on the people more than on the profits, because the entire kingdom values flow out of this paradigm.

As a kingdom business owner, your focus has been, is, and always will be, about people. People and relationships are the fuel of business. How you care for your people is your calling and your legacy. Again, your people don't care how much you know until they know how much you care. Kingdom businesses simply do business differently.

John Maxwell says that leadership is influence. E.F. Parrish says that influence is relationships. Relationships are the key and each one is priceless. In a time span of forty to fifty years you accumulate thousands of relationships. Because of this, we have to be a good steward of our influence, which is our relationships.

A Man Named George

A kingdom business owner, who was also a dear friend of mine, wanted to do business differently. George (not his real name) owned a manufacturing plant with 150 employees. He called me one day and said he had discovered an employee had been embezzling money from the company and he wanted to talk with me about it. I arrived within the hour and the conversation went something like this: "Boe, I know what I could do. I could call the police and fire this employee." Then he said, "But is that what I *should* do?"

I responded, "Well, you wouldn't want that to happen to your child, would you?"

George answered, "No. I would want it to be a teachable moment for my child."

I explained, "Let's make this a teachable moment," and presented some options, including restitution.

We went on to discuss more ideas for what the discussion should include. The employee needed to have a minor surgery, so George would leave the benefits in place until after the surgery. The employee would be suspended without pay and benefits and would also be suspended after the surgery. Part of the money the person stole belonged to the employees as well as the company, so the employee would also need to ask for their forgiveness. In addition, this person would also have to regularly meet with the corporate chaplain for an indefinite period of time. The deal was presented as all or nothing, in which case we would call the police and let the employee deal with them. The idea was that we could present the truth to this person and also the grace of God.

When the employee called the next day, George presented the options. I am sure the person was shocked at the options George laid out. The employee was more than willing to not go to jail. Everything moved along according to the plan. After recovering from surgery, the person came in and stood before all 150 employees to tell what happened and why the employee had been gone so long. With tear-filled eyes and a lump in their throat, the employee tried to explain what they had done, but the words would not come. George walked over and put his arm around the employee and said, "Come on, you can do this." Finally, they choked out the words and shared what they had done. The employee had stolen from the company, stolen a lot of money, and asked the employees to forgive them.

Everyone stood to their feet and came to embrace their co-worker. Not one person stayed in their seat. They loved on and embraced the person, and after that, there wasn't a dry eye in the place. Once they all sat down again, George said to the employee, "Because they have forgiven you, I choose to forgive you. You do not have to pay back the debt you owe." He went on to say to all of the employees that day, "I need for all of you to forgive me, because I didn't have the processes and the systems in place to protect our co-worker, and that's on me." Once again, every person stood and surrounded George, forgiving him. It was such a powerful moment.

After the meeting, the employee met with me, the corporate chaplain, and after the first twenty minutes, gave their life to Christ. I discovered that gambling had become a problem. Gambling leads to more gambling and that never ends well. You will never win your way out of a gambling addiction, but you can be forgiven your way out of a gambling addiction. And that's exactly what George did. The employee and I met for many months and I poured principles of the Bible and living the kingdom life into them.

If we finished the story there, it would have been a fantastic ending, but there is more. You see, over the next few weeks, seventeen other employees gave their lives to Christ. They were primarily an Asian community, made up mostly of females. Coming from a Buddhist heritage, they had never seen love like that, never witnessed forgiveness like that, and certainly had never seen a business owner willing to extend grace and mercy for such a violation. All of these things melted their hearts. God really does take what was meant for evil and turn it to good. In the midst of that negative situation, the Lord stepped in because a business owner, a *kingdom business owner,* chose to love his people. Absolutely amazing!

Kingdom business owners do business differently. It's common to be uncommon when you do business God's way. I am not saying everyone gets away with criminal activity; those decisions are made on a case-by-case basis. However, I am saying that because of the grace of God, many lives were touched and changed forever.

Chapter 5

RADICAL GENEROSITY

Good will come to those who are generous and lend freely,
who conduct their affairs with justice. Psalms 112:5

I learned a long time ago that having friends and having relationships was imperative. In my growing up years, I had a lot of relationships. The Lord gave me the ability to connect with people, and my influence began to grow. Throughout my career, this growth continued. I learned a lot about what defines influence. For one, it involves time, relationships, and resources. All of those things together impact the world around us. Generosity is a large part of how we can influence people, our community, civic clubs, our church, our neighbors, and our family members. It is important to live a life of influence and generosity. I have learned along this journey that hearts can be melted when there is *radical generosity*.

I'll use my family as an example. When we would go out to eat, we might spend seventy-five dollars for a meal. At some point during the evening, I would tell our server that God loves them so much that He gave everything He had in heaven, which was His only Son, for them. But if I had told them God loves them and gave everything for them, and then not be willing to tip generously, what kind of message does that send? A terrible one. They would not care what I said about

God because my example was that Christians are stingy. Instead, here was what we decided to do. We don't just give, we give radically! When we go out to eat, we try to tip the amount of the tab. So, if the meal cost seventy-five dollars then I would give our server a seventy-five dollar tip. On more than one occasion we have seen the server break down and cry.

Recently, I was at a little diner in Guthrie, Oklahoma. I meet there every Saturday morning with a couple of young men who I mentor. One day while we were there, five police officers came in. I told the server that I would like to take care of those police officers' tab. I didn't want them to know who paid for their meal, so I asked her to do it privately, but to let them know it was all taken care of. The great thing about this little diner is you get a lot of food for not a lot of money. For those five officers, and for the three of us at my table, we all ate for forty-nine dollars. Not too many places like that exist now. When it was time to pay, I signed the bill and added the tip for that same amount. Our waitress was in the back of the restaurant when we left.

As usual, I returned the following Saturday. That day it was only me and the young men I mentor. The waitress from the Saturday before was not there at that moment, but she came in about an hour later. When she walked in the door of the restaurant, she saw me, stopped, and pointed at me, and began to cry. She said, "I remember you. Can I give you a hug?"

I said, "Of course you can!" She began to tell me her story.

She said, "You will never know how timely your generous gift was."

She began to tell me how she had been homeless, and someone had invited her and her two teenage children into their home. She was sleeping on the sofa and the kids were sleeping on pallets on the floor. They had been trying to get enough money together to rent a house. She told me that the forty-nine dollar tip happened to be just enough for them to get over the edge, to be able to take the first step in renting a house. The people they had been living with were getting ready to move, so it was perfect timing. I asked the woman if I could call her to find out more about her situation and she was delighted to give me her phone number. When I called her, I asked her to tell me the entire story; I knew there was much more going on. After she shared her tragic story, I went to work to help. Our home church helped her with the move, rent, and other needs. This act of generosity helped to change the waitress' and her children's lives.

I continued to do the same thing with just about every waitress in that restaurant. There is more to this story. A young man that I was mentoring was able to see the impact of radical generosity. He was so moved, that he began to leave a twenty dollar bill on the table for the server as well. Notice, he caught the impact! He began to make radical generosity a part of his life. Some things are just better caught than taught, and that young man caught it big time! Stewarding our influence so that others can catch it is important.

I realize the Lord says in Matthew 6:3, "[…] do not let your left hand know what your right hand is doing," so most of my giving is anonymous. No one knows I'm doing it. But for the sake of showing that we have to be stewards of our influence, some of this must be shared.

God wants us to steward our resources. God wants us to be a good steward of our influence. God wants us to be a good steward of our relationships. I cannot tell you how many times over the years people come to me and ask me if I will connect them with another person. I meet with a lot of people and it's not unusual for me to be having coffee with someone that I have never met before who needs advice or counsel.

Chapter 6

STEWARDSHIP

*It's not about building a big business.
It is about building big people.*

Recently, I was meeting with a young man in his twenties who asked me, "Mr. Parrish, can I ask you, how many people you have in your phone as contacts?"

I replied, "Well, that's a pretty personal question. I would say more than a thousand."

To which he said, "Okay, come on, more than a thousand?"

I responded, "Yeah, multiple thousands." I explained, "When you get old, you walk a lot of miles and you meet a lot of people. I have people that I've done business with, people that are friends of mine, people I've gone to church with, served on civic clubs and served on boards with. All kinds of people have come into my life in various ways, and they've remained connected with me in some form. That's why I keep those relationships and those numbers."

This young man says, "What would it take for a guy like me to get a hold of your contact list?"

My answer was, "You don't have enough money to be

able to do that, nor do you have enough influence. You see, my friends and I protect each other from people that are trying to get our contact information. It's not handed out freely."

Not wanting to leave the young man feeling embarrassed, I offered this to him. I told him that I had probably invested 50,000 dollars over the years in joining the boards, civic clubs, and nonprofits I've served. It takes money to be able to become influential. I've invested a lot of money so I could get to know a lot of people, and in turn, so that I could earn the right to become a friend, or a colleague, or a partner in some level of relationship. I went on to let him know that I was willing to teach him how to do what I had done, but that it would take a lifetime, like it had taken me. If he was willing to learn, then he could build his own contact list that would rival mine, even explaining that he could grow a list twice as big as mine because he was starting much younger.

Few are willing to invest the time, effort, and resources. Being a good steward means we have to take care and protect our influence. We have to choose where we are going to invest our influence and where we are going to invest our relationships.

A Man Named Randy

This story is about Randy (not his real name), a close friend of mine. He was the CEO of a community bank in Oklahoma. Randy was a kingdom business owner.

During his tenure of fifteen years at the bank, he would visit with every single first-time guest. Yes, every single guest. He would sit them down and tell the story of Jesus. Over 2000 people came through his office door during that fifteen year period and they all heard the gospel. He put people over profits. Phenomenal!

Randy would spend an hour with every brand-new employee before they started. He wanted to get to know them, their family, and their values. Then he would share the story of Jesus. He would often spend thirty to ninety minutes a week just walking around. He didn't carry a pen and paper, he just observed. He wasn't trying to discover things about the business; it was all about the people.

One day, Randy was walking through the bank, and there was an employee whose daughter had cystic fibrosis. This respiratory disease is brutal, causes severe damage to the lungs, and ultimately limits the person's ability to breathe. Randy spent time visiting with the employee about his daughter and then asked permission to pray with him. I don't know about you, but I have rarely seen a CEO sit down and pray with an employee about anything; Randy was the exception. In addition to leading thousands of people to Christ through his business, he also partnered with his employees to help dig water wells in Uganda.

When you understand that people are your most valuable asset, you put people first. He and his wife heard about a young lady who became septic in the hospital. She wasn't an employee, and in fact, they didn't even know her. Still, he and his wife drove to another city to see her. She lost both arms and parts of both legs. They met with her, prayed with her, and loved on her, even keeping in touch after she left the hospital.

Kingdom business owners do business differently. It's not about building a big business. It is about building big people.

Chapter 7

BENEVOLENCE

Religion that God our Father accepts as pure and faultless
is this: to look after orphans and widows in their distress
and to keep oneself from being polluted by the world.
James 1:27

Years ago, I encouraged every single client that we had in our Corporate Care family to set up a benevolence fund for their employees. The benevolence fund can be contributed to by every employee simply by opting for a payroll deduction of five to ten dollars per pay period. The company then matches the amount, or sometimes doubling or even tripling based on profitability. Setting up a committee that oversees the distribution of the funds is wise. The fund is for employees in a time of need.

Here is a story that came out of the benevolence fund idea: An employee was diagnosed with breast cancer at the age of thirty-one. She was married with two small children. Adding to the devastating news of the cancer diagnosis was that it was early stage four. Two weeks after her diagnosis, her husband was involved in a horrific accident and was unable to work for seven months. It was an incredibly devastating season for them.

This precious woman went to the business owner to find out if she could apply for the benevolence fund to help her buy a wig since her hair was falling out from the chemotherapy. The business owner said the company would buy the wig, and that she could still apply for the benevolence fund contributions as well. He paid her rent for six months. He paid her car payments for six months. He paid for gas and bought her groceries. All of this was made possible because of the benevolence fund that had been set up.

Her horrible beginning led to a beautiful ending. She completed her treatment and was cancer free. She made the comment that she would never want to leave a company that would take such good care of their people. The owner's influence in her life, shown through radical generosity, literally transformed her world. It also transformed the worlds of many other employees through the years that found themselves in a moment of crisis.

There are so many ways we can influence people in a relationship. There are ways for us to touch people's lives through generosity, through relationship, and through serving. We have to steward all of that in such a way that it honors the Lord and enables our lives to have maximum impact. One of the greatest challenges for all of us will be to steward the influence that God gives us. If leadership and influence is relationships, the more relationships we have, the greater the influence. Just like anything else we have, we must steward our influence.

A man named Doug

One of the most moving stories I can recall is about

a man named John. John had spent most of his working life in a warehouse. He had a little bit of a "salty" mouth, but he loved Jesus. He didn't attend church, but he loved God.

Unfortunately, John was diagnosed with lung cancer and died within weeks of his diagnosis. I went to see John with a man I'll call Doug. John asked us a favor; could he have his funeral in the warehouse because none of his friends would go to a church. Some of his work friends were "church people", but he had a bunch of friends who rode Harley's and none of them went to church. He figured everyone would come if it was in the warehouse. Doug said, "Of course we can make that happen."

John passed away shortly after that conversation. Doug cleared out the warehouse and set up 150 chairs inside. We placed an easel down front with John's picture on it and his Harley was parked down front. His wife actually drove it into the warehouse and John's ashes were in a Harley gas tank sitting down front. Doug started the service and introduced me as his corporate chaplain. I had the privilege of telling the old, old story about Jesus, why He came and why He died. I gave people a chance to respond to the call of Jesus. I told them they didn't have to publicly do it during the service, but I let them know if they wanted to talk to me afterward, they could. Three people came to me afterwards and gave their lives to Jesus Christ. This timing was perfect because, within twelve months, all three of these people passed away.

It seemed like John must have known and the entire service was customized just for these three precious souls. I'm sure there were others who made decisions for Christ, as many people were moved that day, but my point here is that kingdom business owners do business differently. I don't know of many owners who would be willing to clear out their business so one of their employees could have his funeral right there on the site. Doug was one of those men who lived differently, and operated his business differently, because Jesus Christ lived in him.

Chapter 8

I'M THE CAMPUS PASTOR

We have to be willing to do a lot of things differently in order to make a difference for eternity.

Recently, I became aware of the most remarkable world changing church. The pastor and staff possess more influence, leadership skills, and far-reaching impact than I thought humanly possible. Coming from a small 300-member church in the Midwest, this team's ability to cast vision and roll out strategic plans that effectively communicate the Gospel is legendary. The pastor has been faithfully discipling men from both inside and outside of the church for over twenty years. Mentees of his have gone on to disciple multiple generations of people. This church's passion for the lost is unparalleled as they invest tens of thousands of dollars into community events that encourage Christians as well as unbelievers.

The generosity of this church and its leaders is practically unfathomable. With only 300 members in their fellowship, they have provided over 1.6 million meals a year for decades. They have given away millions of dollars to various discipleship and missions organizations, both locally and globally. The church offers every member and their spouse an opportunity to travel and attend a top-notch marriage conference each year and covers all their expenses. They teach their flock how to train their children and effectively manage their financial resources as well. It's simply astounding. The church has also established an education fund, offering a totally free college education to anyone within the church.

This visionary leader, along with the compassionate hearts of his church and staff, have also started a crisis fund for any member who finds themselves in a tough season, needing temporary financial assistance. This not only encourages members to give their time, but also their talent and treasure with matching funds. In turn they are also giving to other congregations and organizations that are making a difference. This same church has allowed another ministry organization to office inside their facility for years and assisted them with financial support to grow their ministry.

This may surprise you to learn of a church and staff who have such a profound vision, passionate generosity, and virtually flawless ministry execution. The minister is a leader of leaders and is speaking with other ministers, explaining how the Lord opened the door for his remarkable story. This trailblazer is one of the humblest staff-focused ministers I've ever known. And yet, most of my colleagues across the kingdom landscape don't even recognize my friend as a minister. His church's generosity, human touches, and leadership skills have never really been endorsed or rarely even acknowledged by the church at large.

You see, the reason there's never been much said about this church, is because it's a church outside the traditional church wall: It's a business. Every detail of this story is true except that it's a business instead of a church. Business leaders have a captive audience for forty to fifty-five hours every week, compared to thirty to forty minutes each week by traditional church pastors. This in turn makes the business leader 8000% more influential with their people than their ministry counterparts.

Come on church, we must recognize and honor these heroes of our faith! They truly hold the keys to the local church's greatest mission field. Jesus was a minister in the marketplace with a team of businessmen who changed the world. Let us go and do likewise, living life with, and making disciples as He commanded us to do in Matthew 28:18-20. This company's acts of kindness, selfless generosity, compassion and discipleship, are impacting the kingdom of God far and wide. After all, everything done for the kingdom of God does not need to flow through the church building to be the church, does it? Remember, the Lord didn't give us all these people to build a big business, rather He gave us our business to build big people.

"So Christ himself gave the apostles, the prophets, the evangelists, the pastors, and teachers, to equip his people for works of service, so that the body of Christ may be built up until we all reach unity in the faith and in the knowledge of the Son of God and become mature, attaining to the whole measure of the fullness of Christ" (Ephesians 4:11-13). The first thing we have to do if we really want to be a campus pastor of our business is to understand what that scripture means.

You can have a vision and a ministry too. It is not just your pastor that does that. You do not just have to be the money for his vision. You can have your own vision. God did not give you all these people to build a big business, He gave you a business to build big people. Period. You are just as called, anointed, and equipped as any pastor. Ministry is all about focusing on people. Want to be in the ministry? Then focus on people. Don't misunderstand me, we have to give our attention to the bottom line, or we wouldn't have a platform to touch lives. The business owners truly hold the keys to the local church's greatest mission field.

I am talking to the business owners here. We as business owners expect our people to sacrifice for us, work long hours, and help make us successful. We want them to have the attitude that they will do whatever it takes to help, but what do we do for them in return? Besides a paycheck, are we there for them in their greatest time of need? Is there a written plan in place of how to care for your people? If somebody goes down, what happens? We have all kinds of disaster recovery plans in place. We have all kinds of policies and procedures to guide us, but do we have any kind of a plan that can operate in building big people?

The story that I mentioned at the beginning of this chapter is called Unusual Church. The story belongs to a client of mine I have been privileged to serve for over ten years. He literally gives away millions of dollars all over the world. He supports over a hundred ministries while blessing his people. Also, monthly, he hands out checks based on the profitability of the previous month. Those checks are not small. They're large. He really cares for his people and he shares the wealth of the business.

He has seven initiatives inside of his company to help care for people, starting with a corporate chaplain, the educational fund, and Financial Peace University. He puts on various conferences. He heads a crisis fund and others. It is amazing all he does for his people who are there forty to fifty hours a week, and they love this man in return. He recently handed the reins of leadership over to his two sons, and just like their father taught them, they are carrying on the traditions and impact.

If we want to have an impact in the kingdom of God, if we want to discover redemptive value in our business calling, it all starts with the ownership of our own vision and our ownership of the plan for developing our own people. The people that we care for are usually those closest to us. They are the ones with which we spend the most time. They are our family, our employees, our vendors and suppliers. It is important that they are also part of the family. They are our legacy and our ministry. God wants each one of us who own businesses to be kingdom business owners.

There are two times in life when people need you; that's when they need you and when they need you. We must be determined to be there when people need us. If our employees are the keys to the local church's greatest mission field, then we are the missionary to that mission field. It is up to us to love them and care for them; spiritually, emotionally, financially, and mentally. Truly this is our ministry and our legacy.

I have said for years that we call what we are doing "the ministry of presence." This is where we literally carry around the presence of God inside of us and we release His presence to search and seek out the hurting, the lonely, and the discouraged. As we walk through all of these companies, we pray before we go. When we release His presence and we truly rely on the Holy Spirit to point out the people who are hurting, those who are lonely, depressed, discouraged, or any of the myriad of life's issues, we are ministering in our mission field.

In the Old Testament, people carried around the presence of God in a box with poles called the ark of God. Everywhere the box went, the presence of God went, so it was always important to have the box with them. They knew they did not want to live without the presence of God. Then, Jesus came to the earth and when He was crucified and resurrected, something truly awesome happened: God slipped out of the box and into us. We are now the ark of God and we carry the presence of God everywhere we go. It is imperative as a campus pastor and a business owner that we rely on the strength of God, the presence of God, and on the Holy Spirit of God. These guide us and give us revelation about each person we encounter.

We must be willing to be available to walk through the building, not as a business owner, but as a campus pastor. We need to make the connection, the touch, and to acknowledge their presence. Check on your congregation of employees even thirty minutes a week during a walk through. It does an employee an enormous amount of good. Remember my story about Randy? That's the exact type of situation Randy would intentionally put himself in, time and time again.

Time is limited and precious. We live in a day and time when the covert operative for Christ must step forward and come out of hiding. Many business owners have been uncomfortable with this thought in the past, but those times are fading quickly. Our days on this earth are literally numbered and may even be over before the return of our King. His return is near! We must take more initiative in the way we manage our business, and how we touch the people that literally give their lives to our businesses and our cause.

If you truly want to be a kingdom business owner, let me share part of the blueprint. You must include loving your people, walking with your people, interacting with your people, not only on a business level, but on a more personal level, too. I realize that is going to stretch many of us. We have to be willing to do a lot of things differently in order to make a difference for eternity. I know this is within your heart. I know you want to leave a legacy of faith, and I know you want to be a good steward of what God has placed in your hands. I also know I have repeated myself, but it bears repeating. The most valuable thing is what you call the most valuable asset. Yes, that is your people, your employees. My challenge to you is this; realize that God did not give you all those people to build a big business. He gave you a business to build big people. Now let's take your people and bless them in every possible way, so that they really are your most valuable asset!

Chapter 9

EMPLOYEES ARE MY MINISTRY

If our people truly are our most valuable asset, then they deserve our focus.

If I asked your employees, "What is the owner's most valuable asset in the company?", what do you think would be their answer? You might say it with your words but do your actions match? Employees are my ministry. This is why I remind you throughout this book, and you probably have it memorized by now, God didn't give you all those people to build a big company, He gave you a company to build big people.

My call to the Christian business owner is to realize that your people are your ministry. You spend the majority of time, outside of your family, with your employees. What are you doing with what is in your hands? Look at what is in your hands: It is your employees. Think about your plan and your strategy. What initiatives do you have for your most valuable asset? It doesn't just happen. Building a kingdom business requires a blueprint. You must have an intentional plan of action with specific ingredients. A vital part of that plan should include a list of desired outcomes. In other words, it requires ownership from the top officer. You will need a strategy and a blueprint, just like you want to build a building, you need a plan to build your people. It must start with you.

One of my clients was a banking CEO and he discovered that an employee was caring for his father with a brain tumor. He was also raising his younger sibling, working on his undergraduate degree, and working at the bank part-time. Add to all of that, the only family car gave out. Another side-note, the man had never even owned a car with air-conditioning. Can you guess what happened? The CEO was so impressed with this young man, that he visited the father in the hospital with his corporate chaplain. He also took the initiative to quietly raise funds from other individuals within the bank, within his customer base, and other friends, and bought the employee a solid, good, used car, with air-conditioning. This made it possible for the young man to care for his family and continue with all of his other responsibilities. The CEO was there for his employee when he needed him most, just like the employee would be there for the CEO when he would be needed for duties at work.

Another inspiring story about this same bank CEO involved three young ladies who were all pregnant at the same time. The women even worked in the same department. Unfortunately, all three of them lost their babies. One had a miscarriage, one was stillborn, and the other had so many complications the baby passed away. Such a devastation. I don't know if you have ever attended a funeral service for a baby, but it is heart-wrenching. When an adult passes away, we all have some sense of the life they lived, things they accomplished, and people they touched. When a baby or a child dies, there is the sense of what life was in front of them that they missed out on. The CEO attended all three babies' funerals within two weeks of each other. The gut-wrenching, heartfelt season of caring for those employees by this employer was something I had never witnessed before. He was remarkable in the way he reached out and cared for the employees in crisis.

So, you're asking, "How do I bring more redeeming value into my business?"

My answer is, "It takes time."

We must be willing to invest time as we get to know our employees. This means spending time walking around your business and really seeing the employees you have. Learn their names, learn about their families, and find out what's happening in their lives. In order to do that, it takes time. And it takes focus. God wants us to focus more on our people. If they truly are our most valuable asset, then they deserve focus. It is the same principle that you communicate when you want them to know about your business, your goals and values. You are intentional to make sure your employees know what is important about their jobs. You must also be intentional that your employees know you value what is important to them as well. In addition, it takes intentional planning with other key kingdom business owners, their input and their wisdom.

Obviously, we cannot give what we have not received. We need to have "the kingdom of God within" us (Luke 17:21). We have to continually be growing and developing ourselves as kingdom business owners in order to focus and give time and ministry to all of the people that work in our business.

Years ago, Frank, a close friend who lived next door, and I had the exact same job in competing companies. He was a sales manager at a copier company, and I had the same role in a different company. If he had lost out on a deal, he would come over and tell me about it so I could hopefully land the deal, and I did the same for him. We competed against each other with great integrity. At the same time, we helped each other. The office equipment dealer that Frank worked for was an amazing company. At that time, it was probably thirty to forty years old. Since then, in the last thirty years, the owner's son took over and it has exploded in growth.

Unfortunately, Frank died suddenly and prematurely. A few weeks prior to his death, Frank left the company he had been with for so many years. He had a new opportunity that presented itself and decided to make the change. The owners of the previous company where he worked helped to pay for Frank's funeral. On top of that, the father and son donated 10,000 dollars each to a scholarship fund for Frank's two daughters. It blew me away to witness the generosity of those business owners. They owned and were leading the way for kingdom focus in business years before I ever knew anything about the idea. They were living it and their example was impressive.

My questions for you are these: How do you spend your time showing you value your people? Do you know the goals of each one of your employees? How do you prove that they are valuable to you? Follow the steps I lay out in the next chapter to be a successful kingdom business owner.

Chapter 10

10 Qualities in Kingdom Business Owners

1. **Knowledge of God's Word.** In the Bible in 2 Timothy 2:15 Paul says, "Do your best to present yourself to God as one approved, a worker who does not need to be ashamed and who correctly handles the word of truth." We have to know God's Word if we are going to have a kingdom business. That is part of what a corporate chaplain does as we begin to mentor business owners on the different aspects of a kingdom life. Learning and having a knowledge of His Word is extremely important.

2. **Sensitivity to the Holy Spirit's moment-by-moment leading throughout the day.** We must take time to listen for the still small voice of God. In Acts 10:19-20 the Bible talks about Peter. "While Peter was still thinking about the vision, the Spirit said to him, 'Simon, three men are looking for you. So, get up and go downstairs. Do not hesitate to go with them, for I have sent them.'" The Holy Spirit spoke to him throughout the day. It is the same for us, the Holy Spirit speaks throughout our day, moment-by-moment.

The Holy Spirit is constantly speaking if we have eyes to see and ears to hear, but we must be intentional in our listening and be sensitive to the Holy Spirit's voice.

3. **A personal, vibrant prayer life.** "The prayer of a righteous person is powerful and effective" (James 5:16). Prayer is much more than just speaking to God. Prayer is also listening to the still small voice of God. That means we have to close our mouth and really listen because His voice can be so soft. God wants us to draw close with Him and be close beside Him so that He can speak to us. The Bible says to "pray continually" (1 Thess. 5:17). Well, how do we do that? Throughout our day moment-by-moment, breath-by-breath, we need to be aware of God talking to us, and us communing with Him. It is crucial we learn to hear the voice of God.

4. **Courage to pray for employees or the company publicly and privately.** Matthew 10:32 says, "Whoever acknowledges me before others, I will also acknowledge before my Father in heaven." It takes amazing courage to publicly pray for your people or your company as needed throughout the day, but it is essential.

5. **God must be first.** You have to be second and others third. Now, some people think that is out of order. They think others should go before yourself. And I say it like this; if you are on an airplane, when you listen to

the flight attendant's instructions during their safety demonstration, they always say to put your mask on first and then help those around you next. They say this because obviously, if you don't have any oxygen, you are not going to help anybody else, so, you must take care of yourself first, not selfishly, but so that you can help others. Romans 12:2 says, "Do not conform to the pattern of this world, but be transformed by the renewing of your mind. Then you will be able to test and approve what God's will is – his good, pleasing and perfect will." God promises in Matthew 6:33, "But seek first his kingdom and his righteousness, and all these things will be given to you as well."

6. **Have a mentor or somebody from whom you can seek wisdom and advice.** There will be times you will need direction from one who walked where you are and understands kingdom business to offer insight and guidance. You may need to add other skills to your life as well. A mentor should have knowledge of God and His Word to pour into your life. "The way of fools seems right to them, but the wise listen to advice" (Proverbs 12:15). "He who walks with the wise grows wise" (Proverbs 13:20). It makes sense that we have a mentor, somebody with whom we can walk through life and bounce ideas off of. This is because success comes from many advisors and a wise man seeks much counsel.

7. **Have faith to stand.** When standing gets tough, it takes faith. "So then, faith comes by hearing, and hearing through the Word of God" (Romans 10:17). If faith comes by hearing, then we must make sure to be listening. How do we listen? We have to schedule a time when it is quiet, when there is no competing noise around us. "And without faith it is impossible to please God, because anyone who comes to him must believe that he exists and that he rewards those who earnestly seek him" (Hebrews 11:6). Faith must come by hearing for us to move forward with any initiatives, with any employee actions, and with any business strategy. As we apply these principles individually, they work together corporately.

8. **Leave margins in your schedule.** Plan your schedule so that you have time to relate with your employees. "Preach the word; be prepared in season and out of season; correct, rebuke and encourage – with great patience and careful instruction" (2 Timothy 4:2). It's important to leave time in your schedule for doing just that. Don't overlap your meetings; leave a little time in between. Often, I have a meeting scheduled at a coffee shop or some small cafe and, say it was planned for 2:00 p.m., then I arrive an hour earlier. I sit and pray silently. Most people think I am looking at my computer or my phone, but in truth I am praying and asking the Lord, "If there is anyone here or who might come in

that needs you, Father, then have them connect with me." Amazingly, He always sends someone my way. People come because the Lord brings them. God knows I've come early specifically for that purpose. If I don't leave a margin of time, I may miss a divine appointment. Usually a person will start a conversation about technology or say something about the music playing. It doesn't matter what it is, God brings them. When we have opportunities like that, it is for us to be "salt and light." Again, that will not happen if I don't leave enough margin to allow God to move through me and make a connection with those people.

9. **Vision beyond the bottom line.** In other words, there's caring and there's culture. We know that you care for your people in one way: you care for them enough to provide a steady job. Beyond that, caring comes in the relationship when you get to know them personally, not just professionally. That is kingdom culture. Mixing business and culture is when you are doing what Matthew 6:33 says, "But seek first his kingdom and his righteousness, and all these things will be given to you as well." That's the culture. You are seeking to value your people for more than just their professional performance, you are interested in their personal lives and the important moments that make up their lives. Employees will follow you because you are their leader. They will follow you to church. If

they see Jesus in you and in your leadership, they will want to know where you worship. They want to know the God you worship. As you develop that relationship and you are comfortable, then you can even invite them to attend church with you. Through all the significant moments of life you are introducing them to the kingdom of God and showing the difference between a business owner and a kingdom business owner.

10. **Have a cause that all of the employees can engage with.** It may be something in the community or statewide. There are so many nonprofits and groups who really need help; getting your employees involved causes them to look outside of themselves. Great stories come out of companies that engage with the community. Kingdom business owners must find a way to get what is inside of them, out to others. If they never see you or hear from you, they assume you are all about work, work, work. It's imperative we care for our people, that we love our people, and that we spend time with our people. Your employees are truly your most valuable asset.

It is crucial that we pray and listen to the voice of God with a pen in hand and paper to write. Part of being a kingdom business owner is passion for reaching your lost employees, those who have never had a relationship with Christ. Your employees are your ministry. "For the Son of Man came to seek and to save the lost"

(Luke 19:10). That is why Jesus came, to seek and save the lost. God has brought people into your business for you to be a kingdom business owner who lives a life so contagiously, even the lost are attracted to it. There is no pressure. We just get to live our lives as an open book for all of whom God has brought to us to be a part of our business.

Again, back to the paradigm that we cannot forget: God didn't give you all these people to build a big business, God gave you a business to build big people. As you build a relationship with your employees, they get to know you and they get to know the God you love. They see how much you love because you love God first. It is contagious, and a joy to see others catch it! Using the ten steps will help you on your journey.

Chapter 11

Practical Steps in Proving Their Value

For those who are led by the Spirit of God are the children of God. Romans 8:14

In the last chapter I shared practical ingredients of what it means to be a kingdom business owner, and a kingdom businessman or businesswoman. Let's take some "bite-size" portions and apply those to everyday life.

Let's begin with "Believe in the Name." I was asked one time by a grandmother if I was a believer who believes, or a believer just going through the motions. Another individual said it like this, "Are you a *fan* or a *follower* of Christ?" A *fan* is a believer in Christ and knows about Him and things He has done, but isn't interested in making it an all-day, every-day, type of commitment. I am a fan of a sports team, but I am not involved with them daily and they certainly are not involved with me. A *follower* of Christ takes the time to learn about Him and decides to live their life to be known as one who will talk, walk, and live it. When you are a follower of Christ you believe what He says in His Word. How did I answer the grandmother's question? I would learn the difference of what I truly believed when my faith in Jesus Christ was tested.

Years ago, I was a trauma chaplain at a large hospital

in Oklahoma City. A horrible accident had occurred, and I was called in to the hospital. A nine-year-old boy had accidentally hanged himself playing cowboys and Indians. He was on the second-floor balcony playing with friends with a rope around his neck, pretending to be hanged by cowboys, when his foot slipped, and he fell off the balcony. He actually hanged himself. There are two ways to die in a hanging. The first way is from a snapped neck and the second way is from suffocation. As the young boy fell and hanged himself, realizing what happened, one of his friends ran to get his father and the other called 911. By the time the ambulance arrived, and he was cut down, he had stopped breathing.

He was immediately transported to the emergency room where a medical team attempted their best to revive him. After thirty-one minutes in the ER, the physician on-call pronounced him dead. It was about that time when his grandmother arrived at the hospital. The staff delivered the news about his death. Immediately and passionately she denied the news and began to speak the name above every name, the name of Jesus. Next, she asked everyone in the room if they were a believer, trusting in God to raise him from the dead. If they didn't believe, she sent them out of the room! This strong woman of God wanted only believers in the room. She needed believers who had faith to help her pray for God to bring him back to life again. I was so blessed to be present and have the faith to believe God would do this. Grandma started praying, I mean really praying! She prayed in the wonderful name of Jesus.

She had no doubt God would raise up her grandson. Not surprisingly, his monitor began to beep, and his heartbeat returned! Doctors, nurses, and technicians ran back into the room to see what was going on.

God truly had raised him from the dead! One hour later he was sitting up in bed eating a piece of pizza. Two hours later he was out the door and on his way home. We had just witnessed a miracle of God through the power of the name of Jesus.

This is the type of belief the kingdom business owner must have in order to be a kingdom focused business. Kingdom business owners will face many impossible situations, and without a belief in the name of Jesus, we will come up short. There will be leadership challenges and customer challenges. In order for our business to give glory to God, we must face these mountains empowered with His name and prayer. There really is power in his name. "And I will do whatever you ask in my name, so that the Father may be glorified in the Son" (John 14:13).

Next is knowledge of the Word of God. Every believer should make this a priority. I implore you as a kingdom business owner, this is imperative that you know the Word of God. As far as I know, there are no shortcuts to learning God's Word. I have been reading the Bible for forty-eight years, and still there is more to learn. Start now, do not wait until you feel like you have the time, make the time.

The way we learn is by reading the Bible. When I read,

I highlight, circle, use post-it-notes, and memorize verses. The better we get at using the Word of God in our own lives, the more natural it becomes as we help our employees use this powerful tool. "In the beginning was the Word, and the Word was with God, and the Word was God" (John 1:1). Another great verse is John 1:14, "The Word became flesh and made his dwelling among us." Also 2 Corinthians 3:17 says, "Now the Lord is the Spirit." If God is the Word, which He is, and the Word dwelt among us, which He did, then Jesus is the Word. Jesus is Lord, and the Lord is the Spirit, therefore the Spirit is the Word. Now that I have you totally confused, let's connect the dots. God, Jesus, and the Holy Spirit are the Word of God! Now that is all settled. You have all of the Word of God within you, because you have the Holy Spirit living within you always and forever!

At any given moment, the Holy Spirit can speak the Word of God through you to others, in any situation. All that is necessary is that we listen to His still small voice within us. We must allow Him to use our voice, our heart, and our mind to communicate His living Word to those around us. Speaking the living Word to others is the most valuable thing we can offer to them. Having a deep understanding of the Word of God and being sensitive to the Holy Spirit's voice is crucial in ministering to employees. The more we stay in tune with the voice of God, the more effective we will be. It comes down to trusting the Holy Spirit, and then doing what He says.

Many years ago, I needed an answer from God about

my career direction. I was praying and asking the Lord to guide me on whether I should be working full-time at the church or continue working part-time outside of the church. The Holy Spirit spoke so clearly to me through I Corinthians 9:14. At the time, I didn't know what that scripture said, I just knew the chapter and verse. I didn't have a Bible with me at my job that day, so, I wrote myself a note with that scripture thinking I would look it up later. Again, I had no clue what it meant or how it applied to my prayer.

Once home, I looked it up and it said, "Those who preach the gospel should earn their living by the gospel." Wow, that was my answer. Because of that scripture, I now had faith to believe that I could step out and go full-time in the church position. Again, faith comes by hearing, and hearing by the word of God (Romans 10:17). God was true to His word, as I stepped out and trusted Him after hearing Him speak. He has always been faithful beyond belief!

The most important discipline is learning to be sensitive to the Holy Spirit's voice. I've discovered that He speaks all the time if I will just listen. We must have ears to hear and eyes to see all that He is doing. "For those who are led by the Spirit of God are the children of God" (Romans 8:14). Every moment, every breath, we must be intentionally listening for His still small voice. The Holy Spirit will guide us, direct us, and speak to us. He is always sharing the truth with us if we only listen to His whispers. Many people say they have never heard the voice of God. In order to hear His voice, we must be in a quiet place away from distractions and train our mind to focus on His voice. For that reason, I get up early every morning. This allows me to hear His voice before the other noises of the day begin.

My challenge to each of you is to put an appointment with God in your calendar and make it a daily occurrence. It must be a priority in order for us to do it. Keep a journal or a notepad handy during your time with God. You will have thoughts that will pop in and He will begin to speak to you. You need to be writing these things down and hold on to them, because you may need them later in the day, just like my experience with hearing the scripture reference. God gave that to me, knowing I did not have a way to look it up. I made a note of it because I took it seriously. It wasn't until later in the day that I saw the scripture and it cleared up my life's direction. Powerful moments happen when you take your time with God.

The three disciplines that have to be a part of our daily lives are:

1. We must study and know the Word of God
2. We must trust the name of God and that He is above every other name
3. We must be sensitive to the still small voice of the Holy Spirit

Practicing those three disciplines will lead you into your kingdom business with more power and authority to accomplish all God has set before you.

Chapter 12

A VIBRANT PRAYER LIFE

We have a multitude of golden moments with our team to model Jesus to them if we will simply seize the moment.

Prayer is essential! Now you may be saying, "Boe, you claim all of these qualities and disciplines are essential." Well, that is because they are. Although I'm not sure anything is more important than the ingredient of a vibrant prayer life. Of course, we all realize we need to pray, but do we really understand what prayer is, and the powerful effect it has on the world? Prayer changes things! The following biblical promises on prayer will help you understand this key ingredient in a kingdom business owner's life.

"Ask and it will be given to you; seek and you will find; knock and the door will be opened to you. For everyone who asks receives; the one who seeks finds; and to the one who knocks, the door will be opened" (Matthew 7:7-8).

"If you believe, you will receive whatever you ask for in prayer" (Matthew 21:22).

"Therefore I tell you, whatever you ask for in prayer, believe that you have received it, and it will be yours. And when you stand praying, if you hold anything against anyone, forgive them, so that your Father in heaven may forgive you your sins" (Mark 11:24-25).

"For no word from God will ever fail" (Luke 1:37).

"Everything is possible for one who believes" (Mark 9:23).

"Now to him who is able to do immeasurably more than all we ask or imagine, according to his power that is at work within us" (Ephesians 3:20).

The Bible is filled with promises on what happens when we pray. That is why we must remember to put His Word in our hearts. If there is one thing I know for sure, it is that His Word is true, reliable, and trustworthy. As a kingdom business owner, we must have a firm knowledge base of His Holy Word. We will need His Word as we grow our business and touch our employees, suppliers, customers, and communities.

We have the rare opportunity to be a minister in the marketplace to those closest to us. If we will seize these moments when they present themselves God will use us to transform the lives of those around us. We have a multitude of golden moments with our team to model Jesus to them if we will simply seize the moment, and that moment is born out of a vibrant prayer life.

Here is an amazing story about a man of God who is the president of his company, and his heart-cry that the Lord would take care of his family after he retired. He had recently turned fifty and been in the hospital a couple of times due to chest pains. There were plenty of stress factors in his life that contributed to these chest pains. More than anything, he wanted to make sure his family was taken care of if he died. Even though he had worked very hard, he hadn't been able to save much money for retirement. He began to pray and ask the Lord to help him with this monumental task.

The owner of his company needed additional warehouse space. There was a warehouse next door that this man was asked to go and check about any available space for lease. While visiting with the owner of the warehouse, he discovered the entire warehouse was for lease. The previous tenant had just emptied the warehouse and moved out. Better than leasing the warehouse, the owner said, "Why don't you just buy it?" My friend, the president, went to the owner of his business and explained the offer. The owner said that he didn't want to buy it, but that the president should.

My friend asked the owner of the company if he would loan 50,000 dollars to him in order for him to purchase the warehouse. The owner quickly replied that he would lend the money to him and then would lease the space from him for so-much a square foot. This all happened so fast that the warehouse owner came to an agreement with my friend almost instantly.

Less than a week later, a commercial real estate agent approached the original owner of the warehouse, and said he had a buyer who was interested in purchasing it. The owner informed the real estate agent that he had just sold it to the company next door. The real estate agent approached my friend, the new owner of the warehouse, and met with him and the owner of the company. The agent made an offer for way more than what my friend paid days earlier. In less than a week, my friend had made over two million dollars! After paying a commission to the real estate company, and paying back the 50,000 dollars to his boss, he now had the nest egg he had been praying for in his hands. With that nest egg he bought several houses to rent out and produce a wonderful income that will take care of his family no matter what happens. God answers prayer!

Let there be no doubt whatsoever, as kingdom business owners, we must be praying for our employees, suppliers, and customers. We must also be praying for our community. The impact and influence God gives kingdom business owners is potentially enormous. Let's all be men and women of prayer.

Chapter 13

WALKING IT OUT

He who walks with the wise will become wise.
Proverbs 13:20

"Disciple Maker" is how I would describe a man or woman who is also a kingdom business owner. This person is intentional about building the kingdom of God inside of those he or she spends the most time with. How does this happen? This occurs during a weekly walkthrough in the business, touching as many employees as possible to extend the grace of God. When this happens, there are those who come forward and ask to be mentored or discipled by the owner. When a person wants to learn how to do life biblically, he/she needs to be allowed to get close enough to see how it is done. Most of what we learn is caught rather than taught. Meaning, we want to show rather than just tell someone how to live a life for Christ.

As a result of witnessing other business owners living out a discipleship relationship with employees and other owners, this set my heart on fire to pursue the same course. I am not suggesting you have to call this a "discipling relationship." It would sound strange to someone, especially if they haven't grown up in church, to hear you say, "Let's go have discipleship time together." No. You simply mention that you would like to grab a coffee with them once a week and see where it goes. It is good to have a regular plan in place. Here are some details about how this works for me. I generally spend one hour with each person that I meet with on a weekly basis.

The First Fifteen: The first fifteen minutes is spent catching up on their week. I simply ask, "How has your week been?" Then I close my mouth and let them talk. You would be amazed how much you learn about a person if you will *listen* rather than talk. Ideally, they should take about seven and a half minutes to share about their week and I should share the same amount of time. From this time period you will glean many teachable topics. Listen well and make a few notes.

The Second Fifteen: I spend this time teaching on a faith topic. This is meant to be a foundational topic and it's short, maybe seven to ten minutes. I give them plenty of time to ask questions about the topic and how it relates to their life.

The Third Fifteen: I ask, "What is the Lord showing you in your daily reading?" or "What questions do you have from your daily reading?" Again, this is when you *listen*. These questions make for amazing discussion. After they share, you have the opportunity to hear the voice of God through His Word.

The Final Fifteen: This time is spent praying for each other. I ask, "How can I pray for you this week?" and they always ask me in turn. By this time, you will already have an idea of what they need prayer for, but you always want to ask in case they have been hesitant to bring something up. Real life issues will arise; marriage, children, business, health, church, and others. Each one is important and deserves a biblical perspective and response.

It is necessary to interject an important safeguard: Jesus taught and ministered to men, women, and children, but He discipled *only* men. There is a strong bond which forms between a mentor and mentee, so, unless you are discipling your spouse, you need to plan ahead and seek out a spiritually mature woman who can disciple women. It works the same for female kingdom business owners. I promise you, if you think this doesn't apply to you, you are gravely mistaken. The devil likes nothing better than to cause a Christian leader to fall.

The overall objective in making a disciple is helping them become fruitful. Then they multiply what they have learned into the life of another person. We have to be willing to let our mentee get close enough to us so they can see our flaws, learn from us, and we also learn from them. There is no set time frame for discipleship to occur. We may meet for a year, or we may meet for five years. It is all determined by how quickly your disciple grows and how comfortable they are in their new walk. I usually challenge them the first ninety days to be in prayer about the person they are going to start discipling. I want them to start the process within 120 days of beginning this process. That doesn't mean the mentor/discipleship has ended with me. As long as they are willing to mentor/disciple someone else then I am willing to continue to invest my time. I tell them this principle from the beginning of our discipleship.

Successful kingdom business owners are always looking for others to pour their lives into. Let's review the three seasons of life. First, are the learning years. Second, are the earning years. Finally, we have the yearning years, where we give back what we have been given, taking us from success to significance.

I made random "deposits" into people's lives for over forty-five years. However, it wasn't until I became intentional and disciplined in setting up weekly meetings, that I became more effective in how to mentor. Scheduling time with the same person week after week is much more effective. Kingdom business owners must become intentional and disciplined as they approach their yearning years. Doing so will move you from success to significance. Allowing people to get close enough to see your life on full display is so much better than just a few moments here and there.

Everyone wants to learn from a successful business owner. They want to know the secret ingredient to success, so hopefully they might be able to make it big for themselves. Whoever we walk with, is who we become like. The Bible says it best, "He who walks with the wise will become wise" (Proverbs 13:20). We could also say, he who walks with the mediocre becomes mediocre. He who walks with a fool becomes a fool. Who are you walking with today? Who do you spend the most time with? What are their values? Are their values the same as yours?

Proverbs was written by Solomon, the wisest man who ever walked the face of the earth. As a kingdom business owner, it just makes sense to walk with wise men and women. Who are you walking with to invest your life into? Are you allowing someone to get up-close and personal to see your real life?

I wasn't smart enough as a young man to ask someone older, more successful and respected to be my mentor. I look at this as the greatest mistake of my life. Proverbs says that a wise man seeks much counsel and success comes from many advisors. I wish I would have heeded those words of Solomon as a young man. I had many of the ingredients built in my life. I had faith, drive, dreams, goals, and ambitions. I just didn't have a mentor. The only reason is because I didn't ask anyone. As I have grown older and my hair has turned white, I have had many younger men ask me to be their mentor. I admire young people with the confidence to approach and ask someone to mentor them. I may have missed the opportunity to have a mentor in my life as a young man, but I will not miss the opportunity to be a mentor in my golden years.

Jesus demonstrated the value of disciple making. He shared His life with twelve young businessmen who changed the world. We should use Jesus as our example and "go and do likewise." In Matthew 28:19-20 Jesus gave this commission, "Therefore go and make disciples of all nations, baptizing them in the name of the Father and of the Son and of the Holy Spirit, and teaching them to obey everything I have commanded you. And surely I am with you always, to the very end of the age."

Chapter 14

MINISTRY IS A LIFESTYLE

Do your best to present yourself to God as one approved,
a worker who does not need to be ashamed and who
correctly handles the word of truth. 2 Timothy 2:15

When someone says, "I'm in the ministry", many people think of that as a title, as if you're a priest or pastor. I have an announcement to make: MINISTRY IS A LIFESTYLE, NOT A POSITION! If you require a title to be a minister, then not many will qualify. We are ALL ministers of Christ's message every single day. So many people are looking for hope and encouragement. We all have the mandate to give the hope of Christ within us to others. Ministry is more than a program; it is people.

After I left the full-time vocation as a "minister", many people came to me and asked why I "left the ministry." It was a joy to inform them that I never left the ministry, I was still serving our Lord. In many ways, I felt I was just beginning my real ministry at that time, saying, "I'm choosing to hang out with lost people in a business environment. I'm choosing to be light in the darkness." It is a joy to choose to love the unlovable, and to run toward people with problems, instead of away from them. I wanted to actually touch lives rather than simply be part of an activity or a program. I was done with that life and my paradigm became impacting people on a daily basis, not just once a week.

We only have a finite number of days on this planet to make an impact and influence those around us. I know a thousand stories demonstrating how we can make our lives about "Him", meaning God, and "them", meaning the people around us. I am the church, and so are you; we must make an impact. Take a moment to meditate on the fact that half of the Ten Commandments are about "Him", and the other half are about "them". Accordingly, our lives should be ordered the same; Him, then them.

As believers and business owners, we have the privilege to be the church out in the world every day in every way. With your business you have a captive audience for forty to fifty hours a week, versus most full-time pastors who have their people thirty to forty minutes a week. Employees are generally thrilled whenever they can spend one-on-one time with the owner. It makes them feel valuable. As a matter of fact, you make a long-lasting impact when you take the time to walk around your facility just to talk to your employees, with no other agenda.

Years ago, when I was working for a Fortune 50 Company, I had a brief discussion with the CEO. He approached me after I made a presentation in a regional meeting. It meant the world to me. I was so fired up that I didn't need to see him again for two years.

Remember, your time and influence, and where you choose to invest it, means everything. Take thirty minutes and walk through your building each week and visit with your people. Whether it is talking about business or personal matters makes a difference to them. People just want to know they matter, and nothing says you matter more than time with your team. Kingdom business owners spend time walking through their business and getting to know their employees as people, not just employees.

Take a moment to stop and think. When was the last time you walked through the building just to visit with your people? No agenda. No destination. Just walking through to chat. Maybe pulling up a chair to sit and visit for a few minutes, without a plan on where the conversation will go. Kingdom business owners should realize how much their employees value their presence and time.

Here's your assignment. This week, block out thirty to sixty minutes of time and walk through your company. Shake some hands, hug some necks, and watch the expressions on the faces of those who give so much for you and your company. Next, make this a recurring appointment that you prioritize more than any other appointment on your schedule. I know you are busy, but this is a sacred time and must never be compromised. In the long run, you will never regret investing time in your most valuable assets.

Chapter 15

GO INTO EVERY MAN'S WORLD

You are the light of the world. A town built on a hill cannot be hidden. Matthew 5:14

I see you: You're excited and ready to do this! You want to transition from being a business owner to being a *kingdom* business owner. How does it begin? Most kingdom business owners start with the Corporate Chaplain program to begin expressing care for their employees. Some of you may have never heard of a corporate chaplain. Anyplace there are people, there will always be a need for someone to care for those people. Chaplains in a secular environment are not all that unusual. There are chaplains in the military, hospitals, some colleges, and professional sports, and there are even times a chaplaincy service is available to bikers at huge rallies.

In a business, it doesn't matter if there are seven or 700 employees, everyone has issues throughout their lives with which they need guidance and a listening ear. Because of this, to have someone they know is readily available is an amazing benefit. A chaplaincy program usually provides on-site visits the same day each week. Consistency is key and valuable; people subconsciously set their clocks to the weekly visits. As a result, your employees have someone to talk to about anything they need.

Another practical step many kingdom business owners have taken is the establishment of a benevolence fund for employees. This provides much needed assistance for someone in crisis. Your business is virtually a small city. In that city, people make mistakes, and they have accidents, illnesses, conflicts, struggling family members, and even addictions can happen. Asking employees to contribute a small amount, even up to ten dollars per pay period, could be matched or doubled by corporate contributions. It is a true blessing when an employee finds themselves in need.

Other programs to help employees might include educational funds or profit sharing. Many companies are now encouraging employees to become involved with a charity or nonprofit of some sort. Sometimes this is set up through the company for everyone to unite and give to one cause together. These all take initiative and work to make them happen, but it shows you care on a multitude of levels. These programs also include the majority of your employees, not just the few you are able to mentor each week. The difference you make with your employees today determines your destiny and your legacy tomorrow.

Chapter 16

A Call to Action

*It is never too early to start caring for
your most valuable assets.*

The CEO of one of our larger clients declared, "Hiring Corporate Care as our corporate chaplain service was one of the top three business decisions we ever made." Having any of our clients make a statement like that is humbling and rewarding. What is amazing about that decision was it took them over a year to decide to bring us onboard. Twenty-two years later the company sold, and the new owners did not continue the program, but my friend started another successful business and continued with our chaplain program. If it was one of his top three business decisions many years ago, he knew it would be one of the top business decisions going forward in his new venture.

Don't allow time to pass before you choose Corporate Care and make one of the wisest business decisions for your company and employees you will ever make. The redemptive value that is wrapped up in this decision to care for your people, your most valuable asset, is priceless. In every regard the program improves employee retention, employee recruiting, and absenteeism reduction. The program increases productivity and helps grow the kingdom culture. Certainly, many considerations need to be accounted for in making such a decision. Involving your leadership team and bringing them along with the vision of caring for your people is a big part of this decision. People really don't care how much you know, until they know how much you care.

Corporate Care comes into your company and cares for your people like you would if you only had the time. The program does not feel like a vendor from the outside, because we become part of your business family, caring from the inside. The business cards we pass out to your people look identical to your business card, adding to the effect that we are a part of your business family, not some distant outside vendor.

We are a faith-based company, but we do not force Christianity on anyone. We meet each employee where they are at spiritually. Building a bridge to EACH employee is tantamount to our program. Also, no employee is ever forced to talk with us. We are adept at picking up on where the individual is at emotionally and spiritually and respect their needs.

Our program is launched with an all-employee meeting in smaller companies, or departmental meetings in larger companies. We roll out with brochures and business cards for all employees, and explain the benefits of our program, answering any questions. We routinely make weekly visits on the same day each week. Employees develop an internal clock, knowing when we are going to come. When we first begin our chaplaincy service, most employees don't expect to need a corporate chaplain, but then life happens (and it always does). They are so grateful there is someone who cares with the resources and wisdom that can walk with them through those tough seasons of life.

Nothing communicates care like Corporate Care. Again, they don't care how much you know, until they know how much you care. How much do you care? It is simple. Pick up the phone, send us a text, an email, or whatever your preferred means of communication is. My contact information is: chiefchap1987@gmail.com or my mobile is (405) 990-0107. We are always willing to reply to your questions, present a proposal, or recommend critical action steps. Reach out to us today. It is never too early to start caring for your most valuable assets.

Chapter 17

FROM ONE GENERATION TO THE NEXT

Our lives are for others,
for generations we'll never see.

Your story is our history,
speaking from eternity.

Those who read what you wrote down,
can now begin to run.

Write it down yourself, or with help,
until your race is won.

I have one last chapter I must write, about a husband and wife team who have inspired thousands of people over the years. After realizing that business, not full-time ministry, was where God was calling them, they asked, "Can you use a business to change the world?" Absolutely! They have since realized that they have more opportunities to reach and impact people through their businesses and that they are in full time ministry disguised as business.

The Hills decided during their honeymoon that Marla would surrender her opportunities as an attorney and that Brian would surrender his insurance business, sacrificing what they were capable of doing very well, to pursue building a business they felt called to create. Soon after getting married, they were encouraged to get away for three days and write out a strategic plan for their marriage, family, business, and the legacy they would not hope, but plan to leave. Ten years into their marriage and business, this couple and their five children had achieved many of their goals of success, but had a huge desire to use their business for more; to make a difference not just in profits, but to connect people to Christ and to impact the world for generations.

They bought a few hundred acres that Brian grew up on farming, hunting, fishing, and picking sand plums, and began building a legacy by design for their family on this farm, and to create a place for generations to return to their heritage. The unique thing about this legacy was that they thought it was only for their family. While that's how it started out, God had so much more in store. Be careful when you pray for a "God vision", not just a good one. When Brian and Marla had saved enough to build the legacy they dreamed, Brian asked God in prayer what He wanted them to do first with the money they had saved. God told him He wanted them to give all the money away. After arguing with God for two hours, then trying to cast Him away because this surely couldn't be God, Brian finally surrendered and realized this was God's answer and He was serious. God was inviting them to give the saved money away, surrender their dream to Him, trust Him, and pick up His new dream for the property and obey as they walked it out. They started saving again, and in God's timing, began building on the property. They built a beautiful family lodge that they called the Legacy Lodge, five log cabins, one for each child, a rustic twenty seat boardroom, the For Generations Barn Event Center, indoor and outdoor wedding venues, 1,000 yard shooting range, trails for four-wheeling, several lakes for fishing and kayaking, and plenty of open space for prayer and meditation.

Since the very beginning, my friends have hosted and blessed pastors, ministries, kingdom businesses, kingdom movies, Christ following politicians, families, and countless others to use their facilities, their land and its resources, to build and give birth to and expand their guests' own dreams and legacies at the Cedar Gate (thecedargate.com). Brian and Marla insist that, "God did not give the Cedar Gate vision to us just for us. He has entrusted it all to us for Him and for others."

Brian will tell you, "Don't worry about what God has entrusted to someone else. Use what you have in your own hands and allow the Lord to touch and bless others with it. It's about stewardship and understanding that we don't own it. He owns it, not us. It's for others, not us. We are just responsible for managing and investing in it. That is what being a kingdom business owner is all about."

Brian was asked, after speaking to a group of young leaders, how you lead in a business when you aren't the CEO or owner. He responded that once you realize God is the owner and we are all called to lead the same way as servants and stewards disguised as a CEO; Christ's Entrusted One. We are senior pastor, customer service representative, sales executive, refrigerator stocker, lawn mower, chief reminding officer, and all other things you are responsible for and have been entrusted with, disguised as Christ's Entrusted One. They built the Cedar Gate to disconnect from the urgent long enough to connect with the important, to serve and impact people, not to make a profit, but to make a difference for generations.

They have used their businesses to train all five of their

amazing children how to dream big, work hard, serve others first, worship God, and give back to the world they live in. They call them their "road scholars" because so much of what they have learned has been through business on the road. They often challenge each of their children with the question, "If you had an unlimited amount of money, what would you do with it?" Then assures them that though God has not entrusted them with unlimited amounts of money right now, he has entrusted them with unlimited amounts of even greater things; encouragement, grace, mercy, love, forgiveness, spiritual gifts, God given talents, natural strengths, and so much more. Brian then asks, "How well are you stewarding what God has entrusted you an unlimited amount of before expecting God to entrust you with the weight of large amounts of money?"

These remarkable kingdom business owners simply get it. I mean, really get it. They are helping a multitude of people dream and fulfill their own family legacy journey through all that God has entrusted to them, including the services provided by the Cedar Gate, the property, and all it offers. The Cedar Gate Media Group, including the production company, helps people get their message out of their heads and into video. The publishing company helps people get their message out of their heads and into print. The promotion company helps people create and promote a kingdom culture. The digital media company helps to create culture and awareness in businesses and ministries through TV monitors in lobbies all over the country. Every one of us has a story to tell, a culture to create, and a legacy to leave. The question is, will it be by default or by design?

With no regrets, these friends and their group of companies have helped me leave my legacy and tell my story so that my family, and their families after them, will be able to continue the legacy. It's so important to write, record, and video your story for your children, grandchildren, and beyond. The only thing that is stopping you is you. What is your story? What is your legacy? Create it, don't just accept it. Finish this life well. Share your story and be intentional about your legacy. Generations of your family members, who have yet to be born, are counting on you.

Come on kingdom business leaders! You have been entrusted people, innovations, and resources for God's kingdom. He has empowered you to change the world for Him, and his kingdom is all that lasts and matters in the end. Can you use a business to change the world? Absolutely! Let's invest every last drop for the one who gave it all for us! Our legacy is not for us, but entrusted to us for others. Let's create, live, and pass it well.

Epilogue

YOUR LEGACY

*Kingdom business owners must always
keep their legacy in mind.*

As a kingdom business owner myself, I realize a small town boy from southeastern Oklahoma, who surrendered his life to Christ, truly has made a difference in this world and will leave a legacy. My sweet bride and I have co-labored in this vineyard nearly fifty years. We have touched many thousands of lives for Christ and have sprinkled salt and light everywhere we have been.

In the last ten years, my legacy has become more and more important to me. I have a legacy of faith for my children, my grandchildren, and even my great-grandchildren. A few years ago, I took my then eight-year-old grandson with me one day when visiting my chaplaincy clients. Here's what I wrote in my journal about the day with him.

Last Wednesday, as many of you know, I took my eight-year-old grandson with me to the OU football Bible study. What I didn't tell you about that day was that I also took him to my clients' offices beforehand. Isaiah spent the entire day with me. He was doted over by the females in the offices, and I still had yet to do my walk through as I do every week with my little man in tow. It was a good day with several employees approaching me about various issues they were facing, and Isaiah didn't miss a single thing.

At the end of the day, as we were heading north on I-35 towards home, Isaiah asked, "You really don't work very hard do you, Papa?"

I answered, "Most days, Isaiah, I really don't, but some days it is very difficult. If an employee is facing a death, divorce, disease, discouragement or depression, it can be a pretty tough day."

He replied, "I think I might be interested in doing what you do when I grow up, Papa." My heart just about jumped out of my chest with joy! He continued, "You must be a righteous man, Papa, if all these people share their secrets with you." I was floored and blessed by his observations and comments. I didn't even know what righteousness was at his age, much less see it in someone else.

The fact that we were helping people, praying with people if they requested it, and simply carrying God's presence into these clients' offices, and my little grandson caught it, blew me away! Finally, he asked me what I had in mind for my company when I got really old and retired. I replied, "We might sell it to another company. I had hoped one of my daughters and/or their spouse might have an interest in it, but they all had their own dreams."

He jumped on that like a duck on a June bug! "I would love to have your company, Papa, and help people like you do!" Wow! I didn't see this amazing blessing coming, but something very special had occurred. I sensed a destiny and life-deposit may have just been handed down. Thank you, Jesus, for a day I will never forget!

Even though that was many years ago, I have continued to cultivate the thought my grandson shared with me that day. Nothing would thrill me more than to hand my company off to him or one of my other grandchildren to grow and expand to new heights. Their walk with God means everything to me. All of my grandkids mean the world to me and their walk with the Lord is paramount. There is something about becoming "white-headed" that gets you thinking about your legacy.

My co-founding partner and I plowed some pretty hard ground many years ago in 1987, when we began Corporate Care. Over the years, God placed a desire in my heart to begin writing stories, poems, and books. It is so important to get those things that are inside of you, out. The treasures inside of you may be passed down to those coming after you. At one point I had over 1,000 stories that I had written in my notes on my phone. I have constantly shared these stories with employees and clients over the years to bring inspiration, hope, and answers to life's challenges.

My youngest daughter, Laura, gave me a wonderful gift a few years ago called *storyworth.com*. It is an app that you load on your phone and subscribe to their service. Every Monday you receive an email asking you to write a story about the enclosed topic. They do this for one year; you write your stories in the app, and they take it from there. At the end of one year, they compile all your stories into a book. You can purchase multiple copies of your life in stories for your family members. Again, legacy is at the forefront of my mind. Your legacy is important! Don't let it go untold. Your story is valuable, and your family and others need to know it.

Something else I have done in recent years is to create 365 video devotions for my grandchildren. I want to enhance their relationship with Christ. I am discipling my grandchildren one and a half minutes at a time with these video devotions. I want them to hear my stories of faith so they may use the stories as steppingstones in their faith journey.

I have already written my final letter to my wife, my children, and my grandchildren. It was an emotional gift that took me several weeks to write. But there were some things on my heart that I do not want to leave to chance after I am gone from this world. After much prayer and many tears, those letters were finished and tucked safely away to be read after I'm gone.

Letters, videos, stories and books, are the legacy I choose to leave my family. They really don't care how many lives I touch, how much money I make, or how big my house is. All they care about is that their husband, dad, and grandfather, Papa, loved them enough to leave clear footprints for them to follow. That, my sweet people, is called a legacy!

Kingdom business owners must always keep their legacy in mind. Business and family legacies don't just happen. It requires intentional planning and a willingness to take action – NOW!

Author Bio

For the past forty-plus years, Ernest "Boe" Parrish has invested his life in building relationships with people. With over forty years of experience as a business executive, minister and published author, Parrish places the highest priority on relationships.

Being involved in the Oklahoma City Chamber of Commerce, Oklahoma State Chamber of Commerce a past board member of several businesses and non-profits as well as an elder in his church he has learned the value of giving back to the community he is working and living in. He has learned that there are two times in life when others need you, and that is when they need you, and when they need you. We must be there when others need us.

Married to his college sweetheart Nancy for forty-three years, Parrish has three beautiful daughters, three sons-in-law and four perfect grandchildren.

Made in the USA
Columbia, SC
03 May 2021